Seymour Justice LLP
(Patton v. Dell)

Simulation File

Seymour Justice LLP
(Patton v. Dell)

Simulation File

Angela M. Burton
University of Southern Mississippi

NITA®
National Institute for Trial Advocacy

Address inquiries to:

Reproduction Permission
National Institute for Trial Advocacy
1685 38th Street, Suite 200
Boulder, CO 80301
Phone: (800) 225-6482
Fax: (720) 890-7069
Email: permissions@nita.org

ISBN 978-1-60156-825-0
FBA 1825

eISBN 978-1-60156-826-7
FBA 1826

Printed in the United States of America

ASPEN PUBLISHING

Official co-publisher of NITA.
aspenpublishing.com/NITA

Contents

Acknowledgments

I would like to thank the students in the Legal Studies Program at the University of Southern Mississippi, many of whom participated in the very first iteration of this simulation. Their enthusiasm and insight inspired me to improve and bring this concept to a broader audience, and I am so grateful for their ongoing support of this project. I also would like to thank my parents and colleagues for cheering me on, and my magnificent editor, Marsi Buckmelter, for being such a joy to work with. Finally, I must express my deepest gratitude to my three best guys, for their patience, love, and encouragement. Without them, this book simply would not have been finished on time.

—A.M.B.

INTRODUCTION

The Seymour Justice LLP file sets forth an innovative, interactive learning module in which students perform essential legal tasks on a potential civil claim in a simulated law office setting. Designed as a semester-long (twelve- to fourteen-week), skills-based simulation, students work as paralegals, law clerks, or junior associates under the guidance of a "supervising attorney" (course instructor) in a small but contemporary, fictional law firm, Seymour Justice LLP.

The underlying case involves Audrey Patton, a family law attorney who becomes the unwitting target of a rival's ill will. This rival falsifies an online dating profile of Ms. Patton on a website that promotes extramarital affairs. Ms. Patton learns of the profile only after she receives a barrage of unwanted sexual solicitations by email from strangers who have viewed the fake profile. The situation escalates when Ms. Patton receives a text on her personal cell phone from a stranger who thinks they are supposed to be meeting for a date, and an angry client fires her from a pending divorce case after discovering this salacious online account.

Ms. Patton seeks the services of Seymour Justice LLP to unmask the anonymous person who created the fake account and to file a lawsuit against the individual for the harm she has suffered as a result.

Students participate in every phase of representation, from client intake, to pleadings, and discovery. Their assorted tasks include substantive legal analysis, legal drafting, and administrative functions like time entry and conflict checks.

While inspired by the surge of cyber torts in our modern-day world, this case file is completely fictitious. Any resemblance to any person living or dead is unintentional and should not be misconstrued.

Assume that any source of law other than the Federal Rules of Civil Procedure that has not expressly been included in the file is not intended to be incorporated into the simulation. The Federal Rules of Civil Procedure may be read in only to the extent that they do not conflict with the other authority presented herein.

All years in these materials are stated in the following form:

- YR-0 represents the actual year in which the case is being tried (i.e., the present year)
- YR-1 represents last year (please use the actual year)
- YR-2 represents the year before last (please use the actual year), etc.

You may download the exhibits from the "Audrey Patton Case Files" section in digital format at http://bit.ly/1P20Jea. The password is Seymour1. As the course progresses, your instructor will release more case materials for you to access through two separate links and unique passwords.

INTRODUCTION

Seymour Justice LLP
Administrative Files

SEYMOUR JUSTICE LLP

POLICIES AND PROCEDURES MANUAL

This page is intentionally blank.

Contents

This page is intentionally blank.

SEYMOUR JUSTICE LLP

4 Equality Boulevard, Suite 2020
Nita City, Nita 88401
(640) 223-4600

WELCOME

Welcome to Seymour Justice LLP. We are a small law practice located in Nita City. We serve an eclectic client base with an array of litigation and transactional needs. Our firm is guided by a commitment to integrity, legal skill building, attention to detail, and a desire to achieve the best possible outcome for each of our clients. We strictly adhere to all prescribed ethics guidelines and follow all other applicable rules, laws, and regulations for our jurisdiction—and expect all members of Seymour Justice to do the same.

You have been assigned to the Litigation Practice Group. Although our firm is made up of various departments and employees who ensure efficient and profitable operations, you will primarily interface with your supervising attorney, who will be a resource for you on all firm policies and procedures. Your supervising attorney will also assign you tasks to complete on behalf of the client(s) of the firm.

Congratulations on joining Seymour Justice LLP. We are happy to have you as member of our esteemed firm and look forward to sharing in your many successes.

1

This page is intentionally blank.

Office Policies

Confidentiality of Client and Firm Information

At Seymour Justice LLP (SJ), we take client confidentiality seriously. All information and documentation we collect or receive in connection with our clients' legal matters shall be treated as confidential. No information or documentation may be disclosed except as authorized by the firm.

Do not discuss a client or our firm's representation of any client with anyone outside of SJ and its employees, unless expressly authorized to do so by the supervising attorney.

Do not copy or disseminate any information or documentation relating to any SJ client unless expressly authorized to do so by the supervising attorney. Do not disseminate any of the firm's policies, procedures, forms, and other documentation with anyone outside of SJ and its employees without express permission from the supervising attorney.

Be mindful of and adhere to all ethics rules regarding client confidentiality and attorney-client privilege. Any questions regarding applicable ethics rules should be directed to the supervising attorney.

Dress Code

SJ has a relaxed dress code, allowing employees to select personal attire in which they feel most comfortable for most daily business. However, when visiting the court or attending conferences outside of the firm, wear formal business attire, which may include a combination of a suit; a jacket with a dress, slacks, or skirt; a dress shirt, blouse, or sweater with slacks or a skirt; and appropriate footwear. In addition, when attending client meetings or special conferences within the firm at which other visitors may be present, use your best judgment in selecting the appropriate attire for the occasion.

Cell Phone Usage

Personal cell phone use during working hours is often a distraction. Restrict personal calls and texts to emergencies only. Adjust the ringer on all personal cell phones to silent or vibrate during working hours.

Email and Internet Usage

Use of the office email and internet should be reserved for SJ business. All messages sent or received in accordance with firm business are to be considered firm documents and must be handled in accordance with established recordkeeping guidelines. Do not conduct personal business during work hours without express permission from the supervising attorney. Direct any questions about recordkeeping policies and procedures to the supervising attorney.

4

Office Communications

Email

You have been assigned a firm email address that should be used for all SJ business.

The following policies apply to all email usage:

- At a minimum, check email twice daily (at least once in the morning and in the evening).
- Respond to emails received from the supervising attorney in connection with SJ business within twenty-four hours, unless it is a weekend or holiday. On weekends or holidays, responses are expected by the next business day.
- Make subject lines specific and easily identifiable to avoid delays in response time from your recipient. Begin email sent related to SJ business with **SJLLP** in the subject line, followed by the client file number or other appropriate subject description (for example, **Re: SJLLP xxxx-000 invoice** or **Re: SJLLP time entry question**).
- Before sending an email, delete any prior message strings unless they are relevant to your current message.
- Remove any unnecessary recipients in your reply. Beware of "Reply All" and responding to messages on which you were blind-copied.
- All SJ emails must meet expectations of professional correspondence. Messages should adhere to the rules of grammar and be free of typos. Slang, emojis, and common text message abbreviations (e.g., "idk," "kthx," etc.) should be avoided.
- All outgoing emails should contain your name and title in your signature block.
- All outgoing emails must contain the firm's confidentiality statement, as follows:

  The above message is for the intended recipient only. This email may be confidential and protected by attorney-client privilege. If you are not the intended recipient, please advise the sender immediately and delete this message. Unauthorized use or distribution of this message or its contents is prohibited.

- Email messages, whether sent or received, that pertain to a client's case must be printed and placed in the correspondence section of the client's file.

Phone Calls

The following policies apply to all outgoing calls made in connection with SJ business:

- Always identify yourself and your position at the firm to anyone you are calling on behalf of SJ. Take notes during or immediately after the call in the form of a Memo to File and place the memo in the appropriate section of the client's file.

- When leaving a voicemail message, speak clearly and slowly. Identify yourself and position at SJ. Indicate the date, time, and reason for your call. Provide your contact information for any follow-up. *Be careful to never leave confidential information as part of a voicemail message.*

Other Correspondence

SJ letterhead and sample communications templates are available in the SJ Forms Bank.

Include the SJ client/matter number in the subject line of all outgoing correspondence assigned to the subject matter of the communication.

Any communications sent directly by a paralegal or law clerk must clearly include the sender's position or title in the signature line of the communication.

Forms Bank

SJ maintains a forms bank on the firm network, which may be used as a reference in preparing an array of documents. The forms bank includes templates for administrative tasks, court forms, and sample documents. Use of the forms bank is encouraged, but employees must adapt each form as necessary to respond to individual client's needs.

All forms stored in the forms bank are considered confidential and may not be disseminated outside the firm or its employees. All client work product remains confidential even after SJ's relationship with the client or an employee's relationship with SJ terminates.

Attendance and Performance

Firm Holidays

Official SJ holidays are set by the firm.

Vacation Schedules

Vacation schedules will be arranged with the approval of the supervising attorney. Any work missed during vacation must be completed in accordance with the supervising attorney's instructions.

Sick Days

All SJ employees are eligible for sick days with the approval of the supervising attorney but may be subject to verification, in accordance with firm policy.

6

Performance Reviews

All employees are given a formal performance review at the midpoint of their initial hire period (the "midterm"). In addition, employees will be formally evaluated again at the end of the employment term (the "final"). Additional informal performance reviews may be conducted throughout the term of employment.

CLIENT INTAKE AND FILE MANAGEMENT

Filing System

All active files are assigned a client/matter number by the managing partner. This information will be provided to you by the supervising attorney.

Reference client/matter numbers on all emails, business correspondence, and time entry sheets, and as otherwise instructed.

Conflict Investigation

SJ screens all potential new clients and matters in order to avoid any conflict of interest that contravenes the firm's ethics obligations to existing, prior, or prospective clients. Conflict checks are also conducted when new attorneys and staff members join SJ, including a screen of their past clients.

Client information is maintained electronically in a database that employees will have access to as needed. Conflict investigation is performed by multiple employees as assigned, with oversight by a supervising attorney.

A conflict investigation must be performed on any new matter/file opened even if the client is a preexisting client. Generally, conflict investigations are conducted at least three times during the representation of any client: 1) before the initial client interview; 2) after the initial interview, but before the representation is accepted; and 3) any time a new party enters the case. Searches must include varying spelling of names and all prior names used by all parties involved in the case.

Make conflict investigation requests writing using the Conflict Investigation Form found in the SJ forms bank. A clean conflict screen must be returned prior to any action being taken on a client's matter other than the opening of a client file, as outlined below. Although some conflicts are consentable, other conflicts are always prohibited. The supervising attorney will provide additional guidance on proper conflict investigations and consentable versus non-consentable conflicts.

7

Opening Files

A file is started for every new client who consults the firm, even if representation is declined for any reason, and for every new matter concerning an existing client.

Concurrent with the creation of the new file in hard copy and in the firm's case management system:

- Perform master docket tasks, as instructed by the supervising attorney
- Request a conflict investigation by submitting the completed Conflict Investigation Form

Include the following items in a client file:

- File Index, to be updated as applicable
- Copy of the Conflict Investigation Form and completed Conflict Investigation Report
- Client Interview Questionnaire
- Checklist for Opening Files
- Additional subsections, clearly marked and organized as follows:
    - Correspondence
    - Client agreements, releases, and consents (including HIPAA authorization)
    - Pleadings, motions, and other court filings (further subdivided, as applicable)
    - Discovery and fact investigation (further subdivided, as applicable)
    - Legal research
    - Time entries and final client invoices
    - Personal notes/memos to file
    - Master Docket Record

File documents contemporaneously with the completion of a task, or at least by the end of the day. File documents in reverse-chronological order. Any time a document is removed from the client file, an "out slip" should be created and filed in its place, so that documents do not get lost or misfiled.

Billing and Time Entry

One of the most important functions of your day will be tracking your time. If you fail to bill your time, SJ cannot invoice the client and the firm will not get paid. Thus, prompt and accurate timekeeping is a critical component of our law firm's success.

8

Unless otherwise directed, you will track your time in six-minute increments. Block billing—in which a group of tasks are summarized under a single time entry and added together—is not allowed. Instead, separately itemize each task and corresponding time.

Precise and detailed time entries are important to our clients so they may assess the nature and merit of the work for which they are being billed. Avoid abbreviations, slang, and jargon. Also avoid cursory entries such as "doc review" or "correspondence." Instead, include better descriptions such as "Reviewed plaintiff's request for production" or "Corresponded with opposing counsel to set deposition schedule."

Perform timekeeping immediately after completing a task to ensure more accuracy. It is difficult, inefficient, and inaccurate to reconstruct the day's activities after the fact. To facilitate good timekeeping habits, your time entry sheets must be submitted to the supervising attorney at the conclusion of each work week.

Tickler and Docket Systems

SJ maintains a centralized system for deadlines on each client/matter, consisting of a tickler system and a master docket system. The tickler system is designed to provide adequate and standardized reminders about important deadlines in the case. When used effectively, ticklers help attorneys anticipate upcoming deadlines, manage their time/workflow, and provide adequate attention to each client. Additionally, each case requires a master docket record to track critical deadlines and appointments (as well as reminder dates). Individual employees must maintain master docket records and ticklers for each client, as assigned by the supervising attorney. Failure to properly manage these procedures can result in missed deadlines or neglected files, which are serious ethical failures. It is important to calendar statute of limitations dates, court hearings, filing dates, due dates, and appointments as soon as the information becomes known. Additionally, reminders must be regularly reviewed and updated.

Tickler dates are to be scheduled as follows, unless directed otherwise by the supervising attorney:

- **Statute of limitations**—six months prior to expiration, followed by reminders every two weeks
- **Trial date**—two months prior, followed by weekly reminders
- **Hearing date**—two weeks prior, followed by daily reminders
- **Filing dates**—two weeks prior, followed by daily reminders
- **Appointments**—three days prior, followed by daily reminders

This page is intentionally blank.

10

Acknowledgment of Receipt and Confidentiality Agreement

I acknowledge receipt of a copy of the Seymour Justice LLP *Policies and Procedures Manual.* I have read the contents and agree to adhere to the rules, regulations, and practices contained in this manual.

I understand that it is my responsibility to seek clarifications of this manual's contents from the supervising attorney, as needed. I understand that SJ has the right to change or supplement its policies and procedures at any time, for any reason.

I further acknowledge that I have been instructed regarding the confidentiality rules for employees of Seymour Justice LLP. I pledge that I will adhere to SJ's confidentiality rules.

______________________________ ________________________

Employee signature Date

____

Printed name

11

SEYMOUR JUSTICE LLP

BILLING GUIDELINES

To honor our commitment to serving clients ethically and efficiently, we expect all timekeepers to maintain accurate records of time spent working on billable matters. Below are some reminders on SJ timekeeping policies. This is not an exhaustive list of ethical obligations or firm policies on timekeeping. Rather, these are some of the most common pitfalls we see in our monthly review of firm-generated invoices.

1. Use detailed task descriptions. Include enough information to allow a client to readily determine the nature and merit of the time being billed. Do not use slang or nondescript, generic phrases like "document review." Instead, opt for more specificity, such as "Review of revised settlement agreement." Be careful not to reveal privileged or confidential information in your billing entry. Speak to your billing partner for guidance if you need further clarification on this point.

2. Do not block bill. Typically, we are asked by clients to bill our time in increments of six minutes. Instead of grouping multiple tasks under a single entry and billing for a cumulative amount of time spent, break down each task into an itemized billing entry. For example, rather than "Drafted Plaintiff's interrogatories; responded to correspondence from opposing counsel; prepared for deposition with M. Casey. 6.00 hours," opt for three separate entries with their respective time allocations.

3. Record time accurately and promptly. Do not wait to enter your time at the end of the week, or worse, at the end of the month. Track your time as you go and enter it into the billing system daily. Attempting to recreate your schedule and estimate your time spent on various activities at the end of the day (or week or month) is ethically precarious and notoriously inaccurate. Be diligent about recording your time immediately after you complete a task.

Refer to the *Policies and Procedures Manual* or your supervising attorney for additional guidelines on keeping time.

SEYMOUR JUSTICE LLP

4 Equality Boulevard, Suite 2020
Nita City, Nita 88401
(640) 223-4600

CONFLICT SEARCH MEMO
PRIVILEGED AND CONFIDENTIAL

Print this memo on standard color paper and attach to a copy of the Conflict Investigation Form. Distribute to each attorney and staff member for completion.

Deadline for response: ______________________________

Requested by: ______________________________

Responsible attorney name: ______________________________

File number (if available): ______________________________

Please review the attached Conflict Investigation Form (CIF) and answer the questions that follow.

1. Do you have any business interests with:
   a. The client? ☐ Yes ☐ No
   b. Anyone associated with the client? ☐ Yes ☐ No
   c. Any person or entity listed on the attached CIF? ☐ Yes ☐ No
2. Do you have any personal interests with:
   a. The client? ☐ Yes ☐ No
   b. Anyone associated with the client? ☐ Yes ☐ No
   c. Any person or entity listed on the attached CIF? ☐ Yes ☐ No
3. Do you know of any reason we should not represent this client? ☐ Yes ☐ No

If you have answered yes to any of the above questions, please provide details below. Any questions or concerns about the completion of this form may be directed to the requesting person or responsible attorney listed above.

____

____

____

Signature of attorney/staff: ______________________________ Date: ____________________

SEYMOUR JUSTICE LLP

4 Equality Boulevard, Suite 2020
Nita City, Nita 88401
(640) 223-4600

CONFLICT INVESTIGATION FORM
PRIVILEGED AND CONFIDENTIAL

Complete this form *before* the initial interview with the client. Immediately after the initial interview, complete a more comprehensive conflict check. Keep this form in the permanent client file. Update this form and repeat the conflict check as more information becomes available. Keep a duplicate form in the firm's Master Conflict Investigation File.

Date: ____________________ Requested by: ____________________________________

Responsible attorney's name: ____

File number (if available): ____

This is a:

☐ New client ☐ Current client, new matter ☐ Former client, new matter

☐ Litigation matter ☐ Corporate/business/real estate matter

☐ Other: ____

For all matters:

Client's name(s) (include any prior last name, aliases, and nicknames): ____________________

Client's spouse (include any prior last name or nicknames): ______________________________

Opposing party/parties: ____

Witnesses: ____

If litigation:

Plaintiff(s): ____

Defendant(s): ____

Insured (if applicable): ______________________________

Insurer (if applicable): ______________________________

If corporate/business/real estate:

Client business name(s): ______________________________

Owner(s)/spouse(s): ______________________________

Partner(s): ______________________________

Buyer(s): ______________________________

Seller(s): ______________________________

Officer(s): ______________________________

Director(s): ______________________________

Key employees: ______________________________

Shareholder(s): ______________________________

Subsidiaries/affiliates: ______________________________

Property address(es): ______________________________

Opposing party/parties: ______________________________

____

Any other associated persons/entities with material information: ______________________________

____

Preliminary conflict check results:

☐ No conflict found

☐ Conflict(s) found (please describe):

Notes: preliminary check only; additional details forthcoming.

Search performed by: ______________________________ Date: ____________________

SEYMOUR JUSTICE LLP

4 Equality Boulevard, Suite 2020
Nita City, Nita 88401
(640) 223-4600

CLIENT INTAKE QUESTIONNAIRE
PRIVILEGED AND CONFIDENTIAL

BACKGROUND INFORMATION

Full name: ______________________________

Nicknames, former names, or aliases: ______________________________

Date of birth: ______________ Place of birth: ______________

Home address: ______________________________

Home phone: ______________ May we call you at this number? ☐ Yes ☐ No

Cell phone: ______________ May we call you at this number? ☐ Yes ☐ No

Email address: ______________ Emergency contact: ______________

Minor? ☐ Yes ☐ No If yes, include information for guardian, including full name and contact information: ______________________________

Marital status: ☐ Single ☐ Married ☐ Divorced ☐ Separated

If married, include information for spouse, including full name and contact information:

____

Children's names and ages, if any: ______________________________

____

Employment status: ☐ Employed ☐ Not employed

If employed, provide the name of company/organization, position/title, name of supervisor, and address: ______________________________

____

____

Briefly explain what you may need advice about or assistance with today:

____
____
____
____
____
____

Have you consulted any other attorneys regarding this matter? ☐ Yes ☐ No

If yes, did you hire their services for any aspect of this matter? ☐ Yes ☐ No

If yes, please provide contact details below.

Please identify all relevant persons (parties) involved (examples: friend, business, employer, neighbor, spouse, someone who caused injury to you, etc.).

Party name: ____________________ Relationship: ____________________

Contact information (if known):

____
____

Party name: ____________________ Relationship: ____________________

Contact information (if known):

____
____

(Use additional space on back, if needed.)

TO BE COMPLETED BY INTAKE STAFF

Client Intake Interview conducted by: ______________________________

Date: ______________ Location: ______________________________

Matter description: ______________________________

If active lawsuit, include following information:

Case name: ______________________________

Court: ______________ Judge: ______________________________

Case Number: ______________________________

Client is: ☐ Plaintiff ☐ Defendant ☐ Other: ______________

Interview notes (include any necessary clarification and confirmation of information provided by client on pages 1–2):

TO BE COMPLETED BY THE ATTORNEY

☐ Will represent (prepare engagement letter and fee agreement)

☐ Will investigate and report (schedule a follow-up conference)

☐ Representation declined by attorney (prepare non-engagement letter)

☐ Representation declined by client (prepare non-engagement letter)

Billing Instructions (if applicable): ☐ Hourly ☐ Contingency ☐ Flat fee

Hourly Rates (if applicable): $_____ Responsible attorney $_____ Associates

$_____ Law clerks $_____ Paralegals

Additional notes (include any deadlines, important dates, special instructions):

FOR OFFICE USE ONLY

Initial and date the following items when completed

Conflict check: ______________________________ Fee agreement: ________________________

Engagement/Non-engagement letter: ____

SEYMOUR JUSTICE LLP

CHECKLIST FOR OPENING FILES

Client name: ______________________________

Matter name: ______________________________

File number: ______________________________

_____ 1. Conflict Investigation Form in file

_____ 2. Conflicts Waiver Letter in file (if client consent required)

_____ 3. New Client Intake Questionnaire in file

_____ 4. Date file opened: ___________

_____ 5. Responsible attorney for the case: ____________

_____ 6. Retainer Agreement sent to client

_____ 7. Signed copy of Retainer Agreement received from client

_____ 8. Authorizations to obtain information signed by client (if required)

_____ 9. Client/Matter information entered into Master Conflict Investigation File

_____ 10. Deadlines, court dates, SOL entered into calendar/tickler per firm protocol

_____ 11. File Information Sheet placed in file

_____ 12. Index placed in file

Notes:

PLACE OPENING CHECKLIST IN FILE AND UPDATE UNTIL COMPLETED

SEYMOUR JUSTICE LLP

C/M number: ________
[Plaintiff v. Defendant]
(Court, Case number)

FILE INDEX

Tab no.	Date filed	Description	Filed by (pl/d/ct/atty/para)
1			
2			
3			
4			
5			
6			
7			
8			
9			
10			

SEYMOUR JUSTICE LLP

4 Equality Boulevard, Suite 2020
Nita City, Nita 88401
(640) 223-4600

TIME ENTRY SHEET

SEYMOUR JUSTICE LLP

4 Equality Boulevard, Suite 2020
Nita City, Nita 88401
(640) 223-4600

Name: ____________________ Title: ____________________

Date	File Name/Number	Assigning Attorney	Description of Work Performed	Start Time	End Time	Hours (round to tenths; 0.2 minimum)	Billable? (Y/N)

SEYMOUR JUSTICE LLP

4 Equality Boulevard, Suite 2020
Nita City, Nita 88401
(640) 223-4600

[Date]

[Client's name]

[Address]

[City, State, Zip]

Re: [client/matter description]

For legal services rendered from [ ] through [ ].

Detail of Services

Date	Timekeeper	Description	Hours	Amount
[date of task performed]	[your initials, unless instructed to include other timekeepers]	[use ethical guidelines in billing to describe work completed]	[round to tenths of hour]	[hours x rate]

Total:

Billing Codes

Initials	Name	Title	Rate
AB	Abigail Brennan	Supervising Attorney	$300/hour
[your initials]	[your name]	[Paralegal/Law Clerk/etc.]	[$175/$200/etc./hour]

SEYMOUR JUSTICE LLP

MASTER DOCKET RECORD

Enter client/matter number, responsible attorney, document received, date received, action required, actual deadline, and date of seven-day reminder.

Client/Matter Number	Attorney	Document Received	Date Received	Action Required	Actual Deadline	Seven Days Prior to Deadline

Update the Master Docket Record each time a deadline or required action is set. *The Master Docket Record should be reviewed daily.*

Recordkeeper's name: ______________________________

Dates of updates: ______________________________

BLANK MONTHLY CALENDAR

Sunday	Monday	Tuesday	Wednesday	Thursday	Friday	Saturday

CLIENT DATABASE SPREADSHEET (EXCERPT)

Client Last Name	Client First Name	Address	City	State	Zip	Open/ Closed
Annandale	Cornelia	432 Redwood Ln.	Nita City	Nita	88404	O
Banderas	Carter	356 Carnation Dr.	Nita City	Nita	88402	O
Barati	Hadise	964 Belle Blvd.	Nita City	Nita	88404	O
Bell	Austen	976 Rosewood Ln.	Nita City	Nita	88404	O
Bentley	Rosa M.	346 State St.	Nita City	Nita	88403	C
Black	Kamron	942 Eighth St. #2A	Nita City	Nita	88402	C
Blue	Julie Jo	567 Eighth St. #4	Nita City	Nita	88402	O
Boler	Destiney	896 Carmichael Ave.	Nita City	Nita	88408	O
Bronx	Hammy	235 Jacob St.	Nita City	Nita	88403	O
Bruin	Joshua	684 Juniper Hill Rd.	Nita City	Nita	88403	C
Copeland	Deanne	436 Carmichael Ave.	Nita City	Nita	88408	O
Craft	Penelope	576 Juniper Hill Rd.	Nita City	Nita	88403	C
Daniels	Carol	857 Tulip St.	Nita City	Nita	88409	O
Decker	Dee	478 Jasper Blvd.	Nita City	Nita	88401	C
Delaney	Kadin	431 Carnation Ave.	Nita City	Nita	88402	O
Duncan	Desiree	5847 Carmichael Ave.	Nita City	Nita	88408	C
Eisenhower	Thomas	748 Juniper Hill Rd.	Nita City	Nita	88403	O
Encalade	Cal	457 Carmichael Ave.	Nita City	Nita	88402	C
Estrada	Karla	700 Timothy St.	Nita City	Nita	88402	C
Feliz	Elif	123 College St.	Nita City	Nita	88401	C
Franqué	Italy	4566 Carmichael Ave.	Nita City	Nita	88402	O
Galanis	Maven	533 Waterbury St.	Nita City	Nita	88408	O
George	Michael	234 Cherry Ln.	Nita City	Nita	88404	O
Goldstein	Noah	8753 Piney Rd.	Nita City	Nita	88404	C
Gorman	Daisha	457 Arbor Rd.	Nita City	Nita	88404	C
Green	Lance	324 Harrison St.	Nita City	Nita	88403	C
Gomez	Kat	347 Pinellas Ave.	Nita City	Nita	88888	O
Green	Justice	654 Park Cir.	Nita City	Nita	88401	O
Greenpeace	Kate	8905 Piney Rd.	Nita City	Nita	88404	O
Hamlincon	Abe R.	765 Jackson St.	Nita City	Nita	88403	O
Hancock	James B.	450 Pinecone St.	Nita City	Nita	88404	O
Hanson	Erica	127 Piney Rd.	Nita City	Nita	88404	O
Hopps	Jaden	543 Harrison Ave.	Nita City	Nita	88403	O
Humphrey	Sarah Cate	268 College St.	Nita City	Nita	88401	O
Justice	Taylor	6432 Piney Rd.	Nita City	Nita	88404	O
Kelly	Zach	247 Sahara Ln.	Nita City	Nita	88405	O

Kirby	Jasmine	986 Best St.	Nita City	Nita	88404	C
Ko	Jeremiah	467 Sunday Dr.	Nita City	Nita	88409	C
Landry	Camille	087 Piney Rd.	Nita City	Nita	88404	C
Larenzo	Lori	4567 Park Ave.	Nita City	Nita	88401	O
Lawrence	Georgina	3463 Abbey Ln.	Nita City	Nita	88403	O
Leighton	Petra	234 Park Ave.	Nita City	Nita	88401	O
Lewis	Mickey	6544 Piney Rd. N	Nita City	Nita	88404	O
Lockheart	Emma	875 Darcy St.	Nita City	Nita	88403	O
Louis	Mack	568 Belleview Rd.	Nita City	Nita	88404	O
Ma	Peter	096 Everly Ln.	Nita City	Nita	88403	O
Mackenrow	Cedar	54 Piney Rd.	Nita City	Nita	88404	O
Maddox	Karen	367 Mockingbird Blvd.	Nita City	Nita	88409	O
Mamber	Nichole	567 Cherry Hill Dr.	Nita City	Nita	88404	C
Mars	Serena	3697 Beach Dr.	Nita City	Nita	88405	C
Matthers	Wilma H	390 Rogers St.	Nita City	Nita	88403	O
Maximus	Sam	3423 First Ave.	Nita City	Nita	88402	O
McLemore	Farrah	540 Bayou Blvd.	Nita City	Nita	88405	O
McMatthews	William	420 Beach Dr.	Nita City	Nita	88405	C
Mendle	Francisco	1849 Seventh St.	Nita City	Nita	88402	C
Mendle	Francois	1738 Seventh St.	Nita City	Nita	88402	O
Mitchell	Angelica	800 Winding Tree Ln.	Nita City	Nita	88404	O
Montague	Leonardo	843 Seabreeze Ave.	Nita City	Nita	88405	O
Neitman	Arthur J	544 Beach Dr.	Nita City	Nita	88405	O
Nichols	Susan	221 Scenic St.	Nita City	Nita	88405	O
Norris	George	2384 Bayou Blvd.	Nita City	Nita	88405	O
Ostepenko	Jelena	432 Fourth St.	Nita City	Nita	88402	C
Overett	Allen S.	456 College St.	Nita City	Nita	88402	C
Pauly	Tori	4599 Scenic St.	Nita City	Nita	88405	C
Pickwith	Aden	431 Bay Dr.	Nita City	Nita	88405	O
Powell	Marta	4372 Bayou Blvd.	Nita City	Nita	88405	O
Prescott	Winston	465 Camden Blvd.	Nita City	Nita	88403	O
Press	Taylor	460 Scenic St.	Nita City	Nita	88405	O
Ramos	Cambry	478 Bayou Blvd.	Nita City	Nita	88405	O
Roch	Shelley	943 Scenic St.	Nita City	Nita	88405	O
Rose	Jack	654 Bayou Blvd.	Nita City	Nita	88405	O
Ryan	Logan	632 Market St.	Nita City	Nita	88401	O
Scott	Marek L.	6414 Fourth St.	Nita City	Nita	88402	O
Sharapova	Joseph	6554 Court St.	Nita City	Nita	88401	O
Simpson	Hailee	6887 Airport Rd.	Nita City	Nita	88409	O
Smith	Calvin	638 Maple St.	Nita City	Nita	88404	O
Smith	T.J.	93 Maple St.	Nita City	Nita	88404	O

Stabler	Tabitha	45 Eagle Ln.	Nita City	Nita	88409
Stewart	Amber	633 Maple St.	Nita City	Nita	88404
Strong	Iliyan	853 College St.	Nita City	Nita	88401
Swartz	Henry	54 St. Vincent Wy.	Nita City	Nita	88409
St. Marie	Martin	842 Landon Ct.	Nita City	Nita	88404
Syrock	Lillian	63 Roseland Ave.	Nita City	Nita	88404
Tavana	Mehdi	953 College St.	Nita City	Nita	88401
Tejaris	Toni	87 Eagle Ln.	Nita City	Nita	88409
Thoden	Jessica	72 Marabel Dr.	Nita City	Nita	88404
Timbeiber	Justin	311 Memphis Blvd.	Nita City	Nita	88405
Trexler	Chloe	79 Maple St.	Nita City	Nita	88404
Troselli	Ian	27458 Irish Cir.	Nita City	Nita	88405
Troy	Gibson	240 College St. #4	Nita City	Nita	88401
Varnado	Camila	7 Maple St.	Nita City	Nita	88404
Venus	Bruno	11 Star Ave.	Nita City	Nita	88408
White	Lésean	349 Oak Ave.	Nita City	Nita	88404
White	Marcus	357 Hickory St.	Nita City	Nita	88404
Williams	Aurora	34 Maple St.	Nita City	Nita	88404
Williams	Claire	696 Lovely Ln.	Nita City	Nita	88408
Witty	Mallory	54 Oak Ave.	Nita City	Nita	88404
Wuest	Rachel	28 Maple St.	Nita City	Nita	88404
Yorio	Courtney	19 Pelham Ln.	Nita City	Nita	88402
Yu	Kelvin	12 Hamilton Wy.	Nita City	Nita	88403

Seymour Justice LLP
Forms Bank

SEYMOUR JUSTICE LLP

4 Equality Boulevard, Suite 2020
Nita City, Nita 88401
(640) 223-4600

[date]

[client name]

[address]

[city, state, zip]

RE: Description of matter (be mindful of confidentiality)

Our file #: xxxx-000

Dear [client name]:

It was a pleasure meeting you yesterday concerning your claim against [opposing party] for defamation. Our firm has completed the full conflict of interest search on the parties involved in this matter, based on the information you have provided to us. No conflict has been found at this time, so we will be able to represent you in connection with this matter.

We will begin preparing the appropriate pleadings in this case as soon as possible. In addition, we will start conducting the necessary legal and factual research to best advise you on how to proceed with this matter. If you have any documents that relate to your defamation claim against [opposing party], please forward them to our team as soon as possible.

Under separate cover, we will provide you with a retainer agreement, which will explain the details of our engagement and billing procedures. Please feel free to contact me with any concerns or questions about any aspect of our representation. In the interim, please accept my sincere appreciation for the opportunity to assist you. We look forward to serving as your legal counsel on this matter.

Yours truly,

Partner name

Title

Seymour Justice LLP

INTEROFFICE MEMORANDUM
CONFIDENTIAL ATTORNEY WORK PRODUCT

TO:	David Andrews, Supervising Attorney
FROM:	Bethany Wright
DATE:	December 23, YR-2
RE:	Doe defendants in Nita; *Norris v. bad_bot*

Question Presented

Whether Nita law allows the use of Doe defendants in the filing of a complaint against an unknown party in Nita Superior Court?

Short Answer

Under the Nita Rules of Civil Procedure, a plaintiff can name a Doe defendant when the party's actual name or identity is unknown but must file an amended complaint with the defendant's actual name without unreasonable delay after learning the Doe's identity.

Facts

Seymour Justice has been asked to represent a client, George Norris, with respect to an online defamation claim. It appears from our research to date that the client can satisfy all of the elements required under Nita law to state a claim for defamation. However, the defamatory posts were made by a social media user named "bad_bot," whose real identity is currently unknown by the client. To properly assert his rights in this action, particularly with respect to conducting discovery, the client must file a complaint. Unfortunately, it is not yet clear against whom the complaint should be made. It must be determined whether the client can file a complaint against the social media user known as bad_bot prior to unmasking his or her actual identity.

Analysis

Under Nita law, a plaintiff may name a Doe defendant if he or she is "ignorant of the name or identity" of the defendant. Nita R. Civ. P. 17(c). Once the defendant's name and identity are known, the plaintiff must amend the complaint and replace Doe with the defendant's real name (the "Doe Amendment"). Nita R. Civ. P. 17(e).

Additionally, although some amendments to complaints require permission from the court and/or opposing counsel, Nita allows plaintiffs to amend the complaint without permission if the change takes place prior to an answer being filed, as long as the filing is made without unreasonable delay. Nita R. Civ. P. 15. The time frame in which the Doe Amendment must be filed has not been expressly established, but two conditions must be met for the amended complaint to withstand an objection from the Doe defendant based on timing. First, the plaintiff must not "unreasonably delay" the filing of the Doe Amendment once Doe's identity is known. In one recent case, the court granted a motion to quash filed by previously unidentified Doe defendants when the plaintiff amended the complaint less than one month prior to trial, despite having learned the identity of the would-be defendants more than eighteen months prior. *Lansford v. Stock*, 200 Nita 149 (YR-3). Second, the plaintiff may not cause undue prejudice to the defendant by filing the amendment in close proximity to the start of trial without good cause. *Lyon v. Roberts*, 199 Nita 777 (YR-3) (holding that the plaintiff's delay in filing a Doe complaint was not unreasonable, since the amendment was filed three business days after the defendant's identity was revealed but nevertheless subjected the defendant to undue prejudice because the plaintiff waited ten months after the complaint was filed before investigating the defendant's true identity, leaving the defendant very little time to prepare for the scheduled trial).

Once a proper Doe amendment has been filed, the amended complaint will relate back to the filing date of the original complaint, provided the original complaint contained a valid cause of action against the Doe defendant. *Laginestra v. Nettles,* 140 Nita 460 (YR-12) (permitting an amendment adding additional defendant, relating back to filing of complaint, as the plaintiff properly pleaded a cause of action for negligence against the Doe defendant prior to learning the identity of the driver who fled the scene of an accident).

Finally, after the amended complaint has been filed, it must be served on the actual defendant in accordance with standard service of process requirements. For clarity of the record, the proof of service should indicate that the defendant is the person originally named as Doe. *See* Desmond Hall, *Foolproof Service* (Nita YR-2).

Conclusion

Mr. Norris can file a complaint against the social media user known as bad_bot prior to unmasking his or her actual identity by naming a Doe defendant in his original complaint. Mr. Norris should make reasonably diligent efforts to learn the real identity of bad_bot in a timely manner, amend his complaint with Doe's real name promptly thereafter, and comply with standard service of process requirements once the amended complaint has been filed.

IN THE SUPERIOR COURT OF
NITA COUNTY, NITA

[Plaintiff's name],	)	
	)	
Plaintiff,	)	
	)	
v.	)	COMPLAINT
	)	
[Defendant's name],	)	Case Number: ____________
	)	
Defendant.	)	

Jury Trial Demanded

COMES NOW the Plaintiff, [insert name], by and through its attorneys, Seymour Justice LLP, and files this complaint against Defendant and alleges as follows:

PARTIES

1. Plaintiff [insert name] is an individual and is now, and at all times mentioned in this complaint was, a resident of [Nita City, Nita].
2. Plaintiff has been employed as a [_________] since [YR-___] at [name of business/ institution]. Its principal place of business is located at [___________________].
3. Throughout this period of time, Plaintiff has enjoyed a good reputation, both generally and in her occupation as [__________].
4. Defendant [insert name] is an individual of the age of majority and upon information and belief, is now, and at all times mentioned in this complaint was, a resident of [_______]. OR
5. The true name of defendant DOE 1 is unknown to Plaintiff at this time. Plaintiff sues Defendant by such fictitious name pursuant to Nita R. Civ. P. 17(c). Plaintiff is informed and believes, and based on such information and belief, alleges, that the defendant designated as a DOE is legally responsible for the claims referred to in this complaint, and unlawfully caused the injuries and damages to Plaintiff alleged in this complaint.

JURISDICTION AND VENUE

6. Jurisdiction and venue are appropriate in this Court inasmuch as Plaintiff is a resident of Nita, the Defendant's residence is presumed to be Nita upon information and belief, and the unlawful actions and conduct of Defendant occurred or accrued, as more particularly explained herein, in [Nita City, Nita].

CAUSE OF ACTION: DEFAMATION

7. On or about [month, day, YR-___], Defendant intentionally, maliciously, and/or with reckless regard for the consequences of his actions, made several false statements about Plaintiff.

8. On or about [month, day, YR-___], Defendant published [describe the defamatory publication about Plaintiff, including the medium].

9. The [defamatory publication] referred to Plaintiff by name throughout, was made of and concerning Plaintiff, and was so understood by those who read the [defamatory publication].

10. Defendant untruthfully alleged that Plaintiff [insert quote from the post]. [Repeat as needed for each false statement posted.]

11. The [defamatory publication] is defamatory on its face. The false statement clearly exposes Plaintiff to hatred, contempt, ridicule, and obloquy because [it alleges something that is clearly defamatory *per se*, such as serious sexual misconduct or criminal activity—state which].

12. Defendant knew the narrative to be false and defamatory but deliberately proceeded to publish lies with specific intent to inflict injury upon Plaintiff.

13. Plaintiff is informed and believes that the [defamatory publication] was seen and read on or about [month, day, YR-___] by [include names of witnesses who read the post; if not possible, describe other evidence by which it is known the post was seen and read, even if by anonymous viewers].

DAMAGES

14. Plaintiff's career depends in large part upon the enjoyment of a good reputation as [describe career and reputation]. As a proximate result of the Defendant's publication of the [defamatory publication], Plaintiff has suffered [damage to her reputation on a local, regional, and national level, as well as the loss of employment, shame, mortification, and injury to his/her feelings].

15. On or about [month day, YR-___], Plaintiff [describe injury/impact on Plaintiff from defamatory publication; add multiple paragraphs, as needed].

16. Defendant's [defamatory publication] was not protected by privilege because it was published by Defendant intentionally, with actual malice, or with reckless disregard for the truth of the matters asserted, in that Defendant had [expressed a desire to harm Plaintiff's business reputation, etc.].

17. Defendant is liable for actual and punitive damages in an amount to be determined by a jury at trial.

WHEREFORE, Plaintiff demands judgment against Defendant for:

1. Compensatory damages according to proof;
2. Punitive damages;
3. Interest as permitted by law;
4. Costs of suit; and
5. Such other and further relief as this Court may deem equitable and just.

Respectfully submitted this the ____ day of ____, YR-0.

Seymour Justice LLP
4 Equality Boulevard, Suite 2020
Nita City, Nita 88401
Tel: (640) 223-4600
Email: [tbd]

By: ________________________________
[attorney name, bar number, and signature]

IN THE SUPERIOR COURT OF
NITA COUNTY, NITA

George Norris,	)	
	)	
Plaintiff,	)	Ex Parte Motion for Early
	)	Discovery
v.	)	
	)	Hon. Manny Rea, Dept. 2
	)	
Doe No. 1, a/k/a "bad_bot,"	)	Case Number: CIV: YR-1: 1234
	)	
Defendant.	)	

To all parties and their counsel:

Please take notice that Plaintiff George Norris (Plaintiff), by and through his attorney of record, respectfully requests that the Court allow him to conduct early discovery on third-party Chirp.nita (Chirp), and defendant Doe's internet service provider, for the limited purpose of determining the identity of defendant Doe No. 1, a/k/a bad_bot (Defendant), who has defamed Plaintiff via an anonymous Chirp account. Plaintiff seeks to obtain the Defendant's Chirp account information maintained by Chirp in order to establish the Defendant's true and real identity. The information sought includes the email address and internet protocol (IP) address that Defendant used to create the Chirp account, as well as any additional personally identifying information Defendant may have provided, including Defendant's legal name, telephone number, date of birth, and physical address. To the extent Chirp does not maintain identifying information of Defendant, Plaintiff seeks to issue subpoenas to the relevant service provider that may be identified by information provided by Chirp.

This motion is made pursuant to Nita R. Civ. P. 1999 on the grounds that there is good cause to grant early discovery since the identity of the Defendant is essential to Plaintiff's prosecution of his claim. Furthermore, while not required at this juncture, Plaintiff has set forth a prima facie case for defamation per se.

Thus, for purposes of establishing the actual identity of Defendant so that Plaintiff may amend the complaint to add the Defendant's real name and address and subsequently complete proper service, and prepare his case for trial, Plaintiff seeks an order permitting service of a subpoena duces tecum on Chirp. Plaintiff has attached a copy of the subpoena intended to be served upon Chirp for the purpose of discovering Defendant's identity or contact information as Exhibit 1.

This Motion is based upon the accompanying Memorandum of Law, Declarations of George Norris and David Andrews and attached exhibits, the pleadings and records on file, such additional papers as my be filed in connection with this motion, and upon such further argument and evidence as may be presented in connection with the hearing on this motion.

Plaintiff does not know the identity of Doe No. 1, a/k/a bad_bot, and no counsel has appeared on his or her behalf. Thus, Plaintiff has no way of serving notice of this motion on Defendant. Andrews Decl., para. 5. No previous ex parte motions have been filed by Plaintiff on this issue. Andrews Decl., para. 6.

DATED: January 21, YR-1

Seymour Justice LLP
David Andrews, Associate
4 Equality Boulevard, Suite 2020
Nita City, Nita 88401
Tel: (640) 223-4600
Email: david.andrews@sjllp.nita

David Andrews

David Andrews
Attorney for Plaintiff
Bar No: 09217

NORRIS MEMORANDUM OF LAW

I. Introduction

Plaintiff George Norris (Plaintiff) filed a complaint against Doe No. 1, a/k/a bad_bot (Defendant), for the publication of malicious and false statements on the social media platform known as Chirp.nita (Chirp). The Defendant falsely accused Plaintiff, an award-winning, best-selling author, of being a plagiarist and a pedophile. Defendant made these statements on Chirp, an extremely popular social media platform that is used by millions of people worldwide. The messages were fully visible to the public, and not just to registered users of Chirp.

Defendant uses a generic, anonymous account name on Chirp and has posted no identifying information that is accessible to Plaintiff or the public at large. Thus, Defendant's identity is unknown to Plaintiff and cannot be determined without serving a subpoena on Chirp and the internet service provider. To appropriately assert his claim against Defendant for the harm caused by Defendant's false and malicious statement on Chirp, Plaintiff must be granted leave by the Court to conduct limited discovery to unmask the anonymous Defendant.

II. Statement of Relevant Facts

George Norris has a Chirp account with more than 1,000,000 followers under the user name @by_george!. *See* Declaration of George Norris (Norris Decl.), para. 2.

On November 30, YR-2, the user known as "bad_bot" began posting a series of abusive messages on Mr. Norris's Chirp account. Over the course of fifteen minutes, bad_bot posted more than seven messages on Mr. Norris's Chirp page. Norris Decl., para. 3. Specifically, Defendant published the following false statements: a) "George Norris is a fraud who steals other people's words." (hereinafter, False Statement 1); b) "What's the matter, George, cat got your tongue? Or you don't know what to say unless someone else says it first?" (hereinafter, False Statement 2); c) "George, why can't you write anything original, dude?" (hereinafter, False Statement 3); d) "Not only does he plagiarize, but he's a kid-toucher too." (hereinafter, False Statement 4); e) "George is a perv who likes little kids. Sick man!" (hereinafter, False Statement 5); (f) "George the perv and word thief!" (hereinafter, False Statement 6); g) "George, I hope you enjoy what you have coming. No one likes a liar or a kid-toucher. And you are both. Your [*sic*] disgusting." (hereinafter, False Statement 7, and collectively with False Statement 1, False Statement 2, False Statement 3, False Statement 4, False Statement 5, and False Statement 6, the "False Statements"). True and correct screenshots of the False Statements are attached. Ex. 4

In posting the False Statements, Defendant intended to and did publish false claims about Mr. Norris to millions of people worldwide, including the 1,000,000 followers of Mr. Norris's Chirp account. Norris Decl. para 6. Any person reading the False Statements clearly understood the references to be references to George Norris, because the comments were directed at "George," referenced his occupation as an author, and were posted on an official social media account of George Norris.

On the same day that Defendant posted the False Statements on Norris's page, Mr. Norris contacted Chirp to file a complaint about Defendant's conduct. Norris Decl. para 7. He also sought to identify the user behind the account name "bad_bot." Norris Decl. para 8. Chirp would not identify the user, citing a privacy policy that restricts providing user information without a "subpoena, court order, or other valid legal process." Norris Decl. para 9. Furthermore, Chirp would not remove the False Statements from Norris's account, although Norris was able to block bad_bot from posting on his page in the future. Norris Decl. para 10.

Accordingly, to pursue his claim for violation for the malicious and false statements Defendant published about him on Chirp, Norris had to file an action against Defendant. Plaintiff's reputation as an award-winning author has been immeasurably damaged by Defendant's conduct. Defendant has maligned Norris's professional and moral integrity with reckless disregard for the truth.

III. This Court Has the Authority to Grant This Motion

Although discovery is generally not permitted without a court order before the parties have conferred, in "some cases, courts have made exceptions to allow limited early discovery to commence after the complaint has been filed in order to allow the plaintiff to learn identifying facts necessary to permit proper service on the defendant." Yale Voices Co. v. Piper, 185 Nita 573 (Nita App. YR-6) (internal citations omitted). Additionally, an appellate court in Nita City recently held that when a defendant's identity is unknown at the time a complaint is filed, it is "proper for the Court to grant leave to a plaintiff to take early discovery in order to ascertain the defendant's true identity, unless plaintiff fails to demonstrate that discovery would uncover the defendant's identity, or if the complaint would be dismissed on other grounds." Farrow v. Windsor, 235 Nita 488 (Nita App. YR-1). Furthermore, Nita Rule of Civil Procedure (Nita R. Civ. P.) 1999 provides that "for good cause shown, the Court may establish the sequence and timing of discovery for the convenience of parties and witnesses and in the interest of justice." Thus, the Court has the authority to grant this motion.

IV. Early Discovery Is Necessary to Uncover the Defendant's True Identity

Plaintiff has no means of uncovering any identifying details of the Defendant's true identity without assistance from Chirp and the internet service provider. Per Chirp's correspondence with the Plaintiff, Chirp will not provide information about the internet service provider or the account user known as bad_bot without a valid subpoena, court order, or other legal process, but will provide the requested information if ordered to do so by this Court. The court's leave for early discovery is essential for Plaintiff's efforts to uncover Defendant's true identity.

V. There is Good Cause to Grant This Motion

In reviewing the "good cause" standard in various Nita discovery statutes, it is clear the law prefers the Court to err on the side of finding "good cause" whenever the interest of justice would be served. Clearly, in this case in which Defendant's identity cannot become known without granting leave for the issuance of a third-party subpoena, the interest of justice warrants the Court's finding of good cause. Moreover, many jurisdictions have found good cause for allowing a plaintiff to pursue identifying information of unknown defendants in online defamation cases, in order to allow plaintiff to meet statutorily imposed deadlines and service of process obligations. *See, e.g., Webfish v. Doe*, 411 Lex. 1236987839 (E.D. Mu. YR-5) (order granting ex parte motion for leave to engage in discovery in cyber defamation case). In this case, Plaintiff has only one option for unmasking the anonymous defendant so he can properly litigate his claim, and that is through issuing a subpoena to Chirp. Accordingly, this Court should grant Plaintiff's motion.

VI. Plaintiff Has Established a Prima Facie Claim for Defamation

To the extent that it is required that Plaintiff establish a viable underlying claim in order for the Court to grant his request for early discovery, a prima facie case has clearly been established here. Defendant's False Statements indisputably constitute libel per se.

Under Nita law, defamation may be established by libel or slander. Nita Civ. Code § 45-64-2. Libel is a "false and unprivileged publication in writing . . . which exposes any person to hatred, contempt, ridicule, or obloquy, or which causes him to be shunned or avoided, or which has a tendency to injure him in his profession." Nita Civ. Code § 45-64-3. The claim turns on "whether a reasonable fact finder could conclude the published statement proclaims or implies a provably false assertion of fact." *Clinton v. Deon*, 259 Nita App. 3d 865, 867 (YR-5). The definition of libel is broad and can "include almost any language, which upon its face, has a natural tendency to injure an individual's reputation or in connection with his occupation." *Fox v. Siegel*, 29 Nita App. 2d 702, 708 (YR-10). When the language itself needs no explanation or context through extrinsic facts in order for the listener to ascertain the defamatory meaning, there is libel per se. The "clearest examples of defamation per se are allegations of serious sexual misconduct, allegations of criminal conduct, or accusations that the person has a venereal disease." *Clinton v. Deon*, at 870. Furthermore, when a statement is found to be libelous per se, "general damages are presumed as a matter of law, and there is no need to plead actual damages." *Abbott v. Lucky Duck, Ltd.*, 15 Nita App. 2d 300, 302 (YR-12).

In the instant Motion, Plaintiff has unambiguously established a prima facie case of defamation. As demonstrated by the Declaration of George Norris and the exhibits thereto, Defendant's publication of the False Statements, all of which were stated as facts, were plainly false and injurious to Plaintiff's reputation and occupation. Moreover, the statements allege both serious sexual misconduct and criminal activity—two categories of facially libelous allegations.

Finally, even if the False Statements fall below the standard of libel per se, Plaintiff can nevertheless satisfy the higher standard of libel. Defendant's statements were malicious and clearly intended to harm Mr. Norris's reputation, and Defendant clearly acted with reckless disregard for the truth. There is absolutely no record or evidence of any kind that Plaintiff is a plagiarist or pedophile. Furthermore, Defendant can claim no privilege for his defamatory posts.

In short, Plaintiff has established a prima facie case.

VII. Conclusion

For all the foregoing reasons, Plaintiff respectfully requests that the Court grant this motion for leave to conduct early discovery.

DATED: January 21, YR-1

Seymour Justice LLP
David Andrews, Associate
4 Equality Boulevard, Suite 2020
Nita City, Nita 88401
Tel: (640) 223-4600
Email: david.andrews@sjllp.nita

David Andrews
David Andrews
Attorney for Plaintiff
Bar No: 09217

DECLARATION OF DAVID ANDREWS

I, David Andrews, declare as follows:

1. I am an attorney at law duly licensed to practice before all courts of the State of Nita and an associate in the law firm of Seymour Justice LLP, counsel for the Plaintiff George Norris (Plaintiff) herein. I have personal and firsthand knowledge of the matters set forth in this declaration and, if called as a witness, could and would testify competently thereto under oath.
2. Plaintiff filed this lawsuit on December 21, YR-2, against a defendant whose identity is currently unknown to Plaintiff and is therefore named as Doe No. 1 a/k/a "bad_bot" (Defendant).
3. Plaintiff has taken all possible steps to locate and identify Defendant to no avail, including searching Defendant's online accounts for clues as to his or her identity and seeking assistance from Chirp.nita to identify the user known as bad_bot on the Chirp.nita platform.
4. There is good cause to grant this motion because Plaintiff requires this discovery in order to unmask Defendant so he or she can be properly served, and so Plaintiff can adequately prepare his case in a timely manner.
5. Plaintiff does not know the identity of Defendant and no counsel has appeared on his or her behalf. Thus, Plaintiff has no way of serving notice of this motion on Defendant.
6. No previous ex parte motions have been filed by Plaintiff on this issue.

I declare under penalty of perjury that the foregoing is true and correct.

Executed this 21st day of January YR-1, at Nita City, Nita.

David Andrews

Declaration of George Norris and Exhibits to Motion have been intentionally omitted from this copy.

AUDREY PATTON CASE FILES

In addition to the materials contained in this section, you will be working with a completed intake questionnaire, an interoffice email and intake interview transcript, and, later, a retainer agreement.

These materials will be timed for release at two different moments in the course. Your instructor will provide you with the URLs and unique passwords so you may download and save these files.

You may download the exhibits from this section in digital format at http://bit.ly/1P20Jea. The password is Seymour1.

AUDREY LEE PATTON

33 Mockingbird Boulevard
Nita City, Nita 88409

Education

Nita University School of Law
JD (YR-11)
Honors: *Summa Cum Laude*; Excellence in Family Law Award; Community Service Award; Dean's List
Activities: *Nita Law Review,* YR-11 to YR-13, Managing Editor, Volume 40; Legal Intern with Nita City Access to Justice Commission

Nita University
BA, English (YR-14)
Honors: Phi Beta Kappa, President's List (YR-17 to YR-14)

Employment

Merritt & Levy, LLP (YR-10 to present)

Partner, Family Law Group
Represent clients in all aspects of domestic relations cases in litigation and alternative dispute resolution settings, including the negotiation and preparation of prenuptial, postnuptial, and separation agreements; contested and uncontested divorce; alimony; paternity; and child custody cases

Hon. Tom Schepard (YR-11 to YR-10)
Law Clerk, Nita Supreme Court

Publications

"Ethical Utilization of Nonlawyers in Family Law," 50 *Nita L. Rev.* 19 (YR-1)
"Criminal Conversation in a Digital Age," *Nita Family Law Journal*, February YR-3
"State of Affairs in Nita City: Contemporary Heartbalm Statutes," *Nita Lawyer*, June YR-3

Professional Associations and Memberships

Nita State Bar Association
Nita City Collaborative Law Association
Nita Association of Family Law Mediators

Merritt & Levy, LLP

| Our Team | Our Services | Our Firm

Contact

(640) 222-8449
21 Court Street
Nita City, Nita 88401
audrey.patton@merrittlevy.com

Awards

» NAFL Superstar in Family Law (YR-1)

» NCBA Most Oustanding Woman in Law (YR-2)

Recent Publications

"Ethical Utilization of Nonlawyers in Family Law," 50 Nita L. Rev. 19 (YR-1).

"Criminal Conversation in a Digital Age," Nita Family Law Journal, February YR-1.

"State of Affairs in Nita City: Contemporary Heartbalm Statutes," Nita Lawyer, June YR-3.

Audrey Lee Patton

Partner

Audrey Lee Patton is a partner in the Family Law Group at Merritt & Levy, LLP, where she has practiced for the last ten years. Prior to joining Merritt & Levy, Audrey clerked for the Honorable Tom Schepard of the Nita Supreme Court.

She is widely recognized for developing creative, customized solutions for her clients. Audrey is a fierce competitor and zealous advocate, well-respected by her peers. She is a frequent CLE presenter on trends in family law at law firms across Nita City and was selected for the coveted Superstar in Family Law award from the National Association of Family Lawyers in YR-1.

Audrey is actively involved in numerous legal associations, including the Nita State Bar Association, the Nita City Collaborative Law Association, and the Nita Association of Family Law Mediators. In YR-2, Audrey was honored by the Nita City Bar Association as the Most Outstanding Woman in Law. Additionally, she has been a featured speaker around the country on the resurgence of so-called "heartbalm" statutes.

Audrey received her JD from Nita University School of Law, where she graduated summa cum laude and interned with the Nita City Access to Justice Commission. She received her undergraduate degree at Nita University, where she was inducted into Phi Beta Kappa.

Audrey is admitted to practice law in Nita. She lives in Nita City, with her husband Charlie and twin daughters, Marilyn and Amelia.

National Association of Family Lawyers **August YR-1**

The National Association of Family Lawyers (NAFL) is pleased to announce this year's list of **Superstars in Family Law**. Inclusion in this ranking is widely considered a crown jewel of peer-recognized excellence in family law. This year's awardees are recognized for their commitment to zealous advocacy on behalf of their clients while maintaining the gold standard for civility and integrity within the legal profession. The professionals in this year's list are among fewer than 1 percent of family law attorneys in the entire State of Nita who have received this honor. Congratulations to them all!

YR-1 Superstars include:

- John LaRocha, Partner, Cullen Armstrong & Associates
- Aicha London, Associate, Cullen Armstrong & Associates
- Robby Pauer, Law Offices of Robby Pauer
- Audrey Lee Patton, Partner, Merritt & Levy LLP
- Elizabeth Wilson, Partner, Wilson Triolo & Dwight LLP

This year, NAFL also recognizes a few promising attorneys with the "Family Lawyer—Honorable Mention" distinction. While not quite satisfying the rigorous criteria for selection as a Superstar, these up-and-comers are likely to land on a future list.

- Bella Boyd, Senior Associate, Newman Sayre & Weinberg LLP
- Lana Dean, Associate, Harrison Forrest LLP
- Jared Dell, Senior Associate, Schepard Lane LLP

RateYourAttorney.Nita

Audrey Patton

☆☆☆☆☆

(0 out of 5 stars)
2 reviews

Audrey Patton
Partner, Family Law
Merritt & Levy LLP
Nita City, Nita
Licensed for 11 years

Reviews:

0/5 stars

Liar, cheater, unethical. She'll probably try to steal your spouse, since she's into that kind of thing.

Posted by Anonymous
Day-01, YR-0, 2:31 pm

0/5 stars

I am so upset and feel like I need to warn everyone. I was a client until this morning. Audrey sat with me for a full hour after a deposition when I found out that my spouse of fifteen years had been cheating on me with our babysitter. She pretended to care, gave me tissues, held my hand, told me it would be ok. "We'll fix this," she said. She told me I could sue the babysitter, that there was a way to hold the other woman responsible for the harm she caused. Audrey presented herself like a great champion of innocent spouses. But I found out that she is a cheater herself! She has a profile on Rendezvous! You can't be more blatant than that. I knew lawyers had a reputation for being liars, but I can't believe the act she put on. I really trusted her. Now I'm just disgusted. Do yourself a favor. Find another attorney!

Posted by Anonymous
Day-01, YR-0, 1:15 pm

Unified Message System Alert

SENT: Day-01, YR-0 11:46 AM
TO: Audrey Patton
RE: Voicemail from Unknown Caller (21 seconds)
ATTACHMENT: soundfile.mp3

Message Preview

Hi Audrey. This is Taylor Cabello. I am calling to let you know that I will no longer be needing your services in my divorce. I am married to a cheater. I don't want to be represented by one. You really should be ashamed of yourself. I will be in touch soon with my new attorney to get all my files. Do not call me back. <end of message>

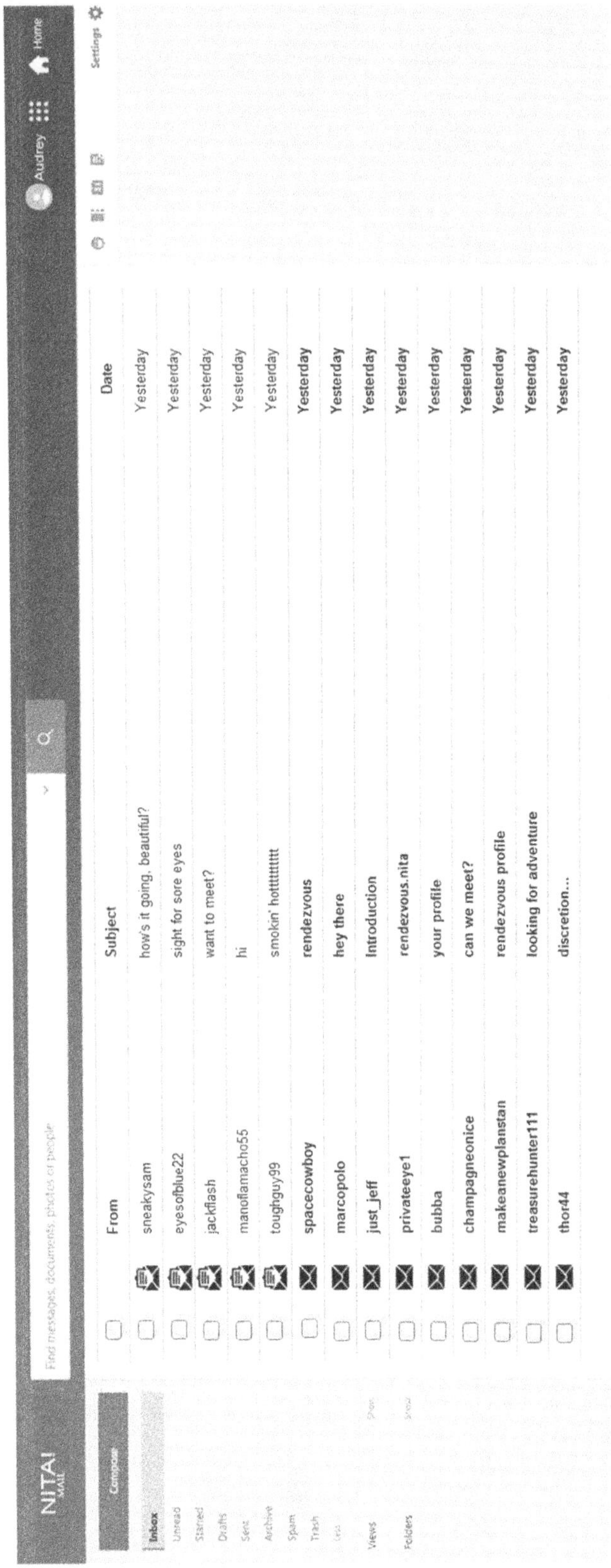
NITA! MAIL
Find messages, documents, photos or people
Audrey
Home
Compose
Inbox
Unread
Starred
Drafts
Sent
Archive
Spam
Trash
Views
Folders
Settings
From
Subject
Date
sneakysam how's it going, beautiful? Yesterday
eyesofblue22 sight for sore eyes Yesterday
jackflash want to meet? Yesterday
manoflamacho55 hi Yesterday
toughguy99 smokin' hotttttttttt Yesterday
spacecowboy rendezvous Yesterday
marcopolo hey there Yesterday
just_jeff Introduction Yesterday
privateeye1 rendezvous.nita Yesterday
bubba your profile Yesterday
champagneonice can we meet? Yesterday
makeanewplanstan rendezvous profile Yesterday
treasurehunter111 looking for adventure Yesterday
thor44 discretion... Yesterday

FROM: makeanewplanstan@rendezvous.nita
DATE: Day-01, YR-0 at 9:06 AM
TO: audrey.patton@merrittlevy.nita
SUBJECT: Re: re: rendezvous profile

What kind of game are you running? It's your email address, your name, and it's your face from your law firm website.

Cold feet? Maybe I can help with that.

> On Day-01, YR-0 at 8:47 AM, audrey.patton@merrittlevy.nita wrote:
> Stan:
>
> This is a fake profile. Someone has posted my contact information, but I don't have an account on this
> website. I'm receiving lots of messages right now from this site. Can you please report it?
>
> Sincerely,
> ALP

>> On Day-01, YR-0 at 7:57 AM, makeanewplanstan@rendezvous.nita wrote:
>> Your profile is intriguing. Like the song says, there's a lot of different ways to leave your lover. Can I
>> help with that?

>> Stan the man (with a plan)

FROM: Audrey Patton
DATE: Day-01, YR-0 at 8:45 AM
TO: thor44@rendezvous.nita
SUBJECT: Re: discretion . . .

Hi Thor:

I'm sorry, but I think you've been taken in by a fake profile. I don't have an account on this website. Can you please report it?

Sincerely,
ALP

> On Day-01, YR-0 at 7:31 AM, thor44@rendezvous.nita wrote:
> Hi there,
>
> I am new at this and feeling a little awkward . . . but I saw your profile on rendezvous. I would really
> like to get to know you better. Can we try chatting by phone? Email can be so impersonal. And
> it leaves a paper trail . . . if you're up for it, please write me back.
>
> -thor44

FROM: Audrey Patton
DATE: Day-01, YR-0 at 8:45 AM
TO: treasurehunter111@rendezvous.nita
SUBJECT: Re: looking for adventure

Hi Treasurehunter111:

This is a fake profile. Someone has posted my contact information, but I don't have an account on this website. Can you please report it?

Sincerely,
ALP

> On Day-01, YR-0 at 7:33 AM, treasurehunter111@rendezvous.nita wrote:

> I saw your profile and I want to know more. Please message me back. I'm looking forward to the
> adventures we can have together.
>
> -T

1:42 P.M.
72%
Messages
U
Unknown
Details
Hi -I'm here. Where are you? I don't see you anywhere...don't tell me cold feet. lol
I'm sorry...who is this?
It's Jeff...from rendezvous...we said 11:00, right? at the Parisian? Did I get the day wrong?
Oh no. This has been some kind of mistake. Someone has created a fake profile with my information.
Send

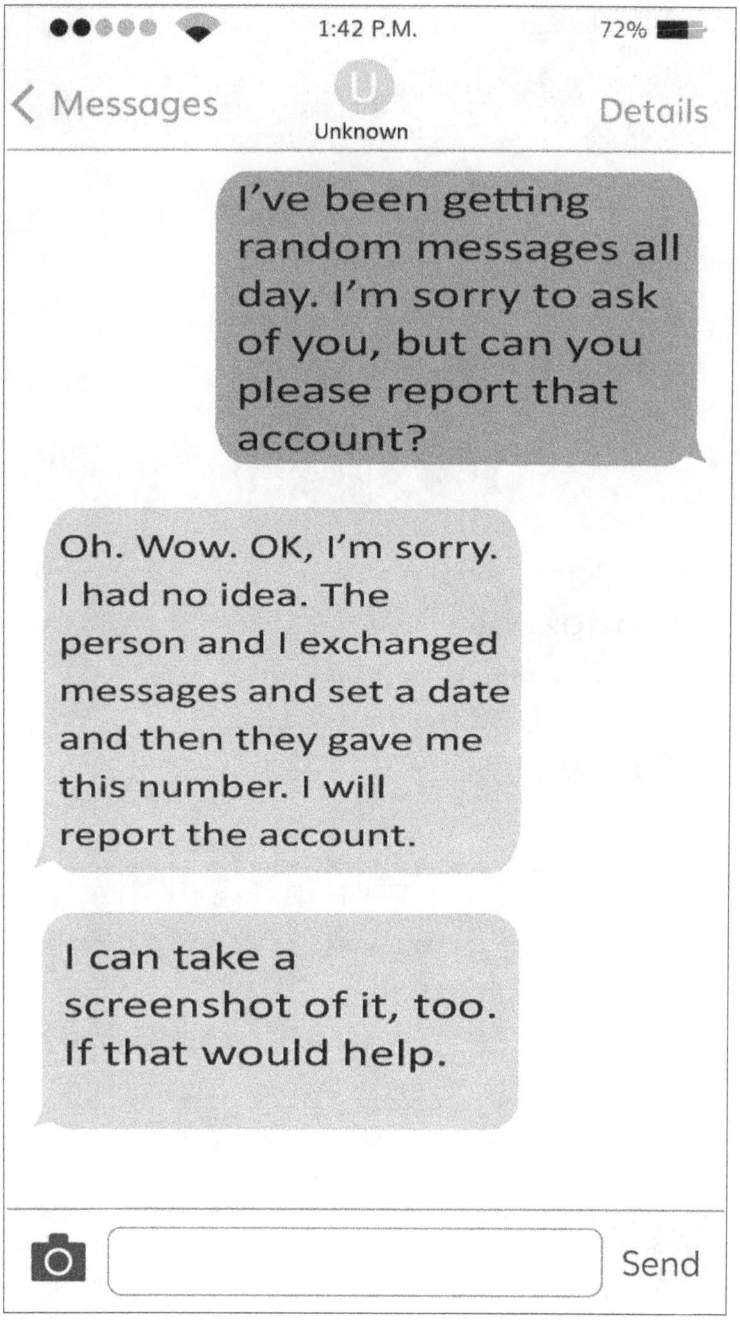
1:42 P.M.
72%
Messages
U
Unknown
Details
I've been getting random messages all day. I'm sorry to ask of you, but can you please report that account?
Oh. Wow. OK, I'm sorry. I had no idea. The person and I exchanged messages and set a date and then they gave me this number. I will report the account.
I can take a screenshot of it, too. If that would help.
Send

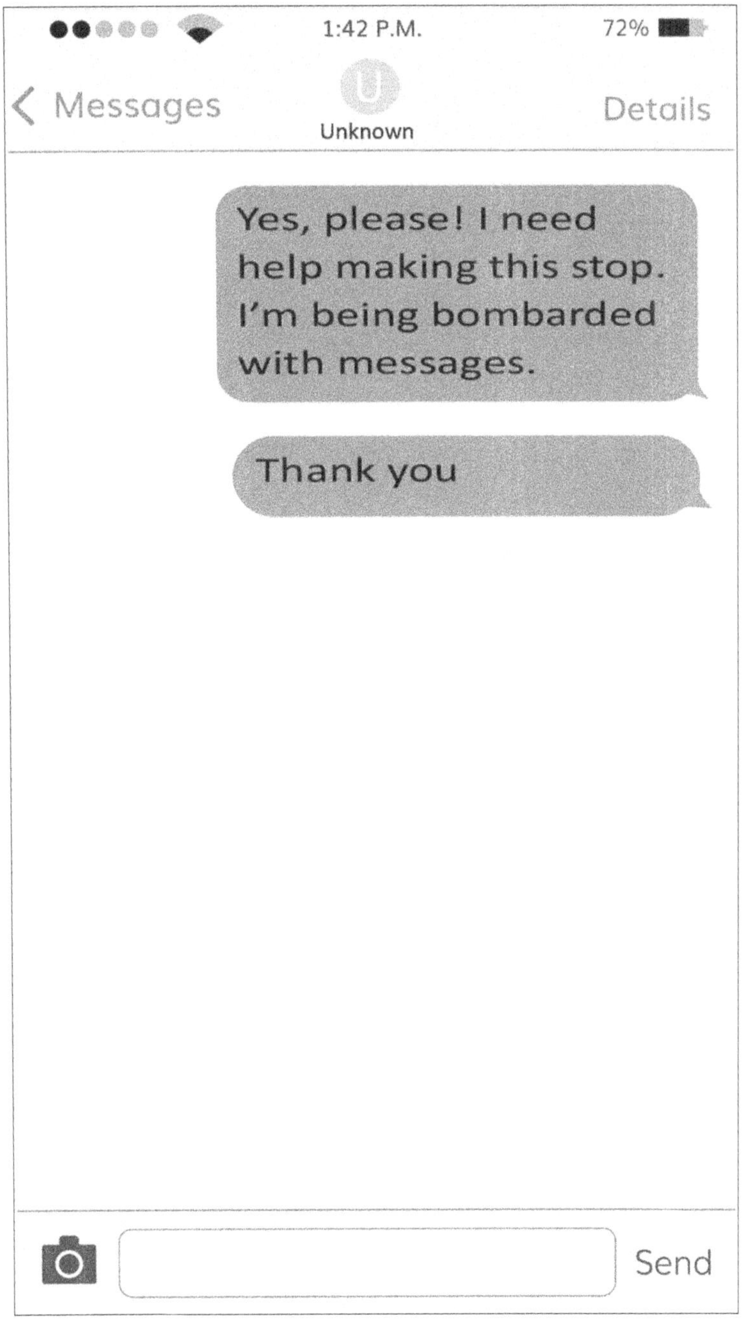

1:42 P.M.
72%
Messages
U
Unknown
Details
Yes, please! I need help making this stop. I'm being bombarded with messages.
Thank you
Send

ren·dez·vous /ˈrändəˌvo͞o, ˈrändāˌvo͞o/

Meet your *other* significant other.

The basics . . .

Name:	Audrey_Patton_Paramour
Age:	middle-aged
Occupation:	attorney
Status:	married, but in name only
Body Type:	we'll call it "curvy"
Likes:	always being right, telling white lies, sneaking around, and food!!!
Dislikes:	losing, dieting, being married

A little more . . .

I may seem like a goody two-shoes. Most people think I'm sweet. But trust me, there are two sides to this coin. I will do whatever it takes to get my way. Cheating . . . it's in my DNA. My poor husband has no idea the games I can play. What he doesn't know might hurt him, but who cares? As long as I do what I want, I'll be happy. If you're up for a rendezvous, get in touch. You can contact me anytime at audrey.patton@merrittlevy.nita. Hope to hear from you soon!

ren·dez·vous /ˈrändəˌvo͞o, ˈrändāˌvo͞o/

Requests for Account Information

Rendezvous.nita (Rendezvous) respects the privacy of its users. At times, we may receive a request to produce user data in response to legal proceedings. When we receive such a request, our legal team carefully reviews the request to make sure it complies with applicable legal requirements and Rendezvous policies. When necessary, Rendezvous will challenge requests for information that are too broad, vague, or inconsistent with applicable laws.

Requests for user account information should be directed to the Legal Compliance Office of Rendezvous in Nita City, Nita. Rendezvous will respond to valid legal process issued in compliance with applicable law. However, nonpublic information about users will not be released to any individual or agency unless required by subpoena, court order, or other valid legal process.

Rendezvous's policy is to notify users of requests for their account information prior to disclosure of any nonpublic user information, unless notification is prohibited by law. Exceptions to prior notice may be made in exigent circumstances, which typically involve imminent risk of serious bodily injury or death to any person. Requests for information under exigent circumstances must contain a detailed description of the emergency and an explanation of how the requested information might prevent the harm. We will limit disclosure in exigent circumstances to the information we believe would help prevent the harm, unless otherwise required by law.

If prior notice is prohibited by law or exigent circumstances, Rendezvous will provide notice to the user after disclosure once any legal prohibition against disclosure has been lifted.

All requests should be made on official letterhead of a law enforcement agency or other legal authority and submitted to our Legal Compliance Office. We are unable to process requests that are overly broad or vague. When requesting user account information, please include:

- The username of the account in question
- Sufficient details about the information being requested
- A valid subpoena, court order, or documentation of other valid legal process
- A valid email address or other valid contact information

Contact Information

Rendezvous
Attn: Legal Compliance Office
77 Wright Ave.
Nita City, Nita 88401
(640) 222-5678
legal@rendezvous.nita

Delayed-Access Research Files

These research files can be accessed and downloaded as electronic files. At the appropriate time in the course, your instructor will advise you of the URL and password.

Problems

Problem 1: Firm Orientation

Welcome to Seymour Justice LLP. Whether you are joining us as a paralegal, law clerk, or junior attorney, we are happy to have you on our team. Take some time to review all the introductory materials that have been provided to you, especially the *Policies and Procedures Manual*. Pay special attention to the policies on opening client matters/client intake, file management, and time entry.

You are a member of the civil litigation unit, which means you will work with clients on civil disputes that may end up in trial.

If you have any questions, ask your supervising attorney for guidance.

Problem 2: Prospective Client Intake

Our firm has been asked to retain a new client named Audrey Patton. She will be coming into the firm shortly for an intake interview. Review the Client Intake Questionnaire and Conflict Check Forms and await further instruction from your supervising attorney.

Problem 3: Conflict Check /Opening Client File/Time Entry

The managing partner believes that Audrey Patton has a strong case and is eager for Seymour Justice to represent her. The conflicts department must first complete the conflict screen based on the information available to be sure the firm may represent Ms. Patton.

Once you have been notified that the conflict check has cleared, open a new client file. The supervising attorney will provide you with the client/matter (c/m) number to be used in connection with Ms. Patton's case going forward. Update the Checklist for Opening Files and the File Index Form, as appropriate. Review the *Policies and Procedures Manual* (manual) for additional guidance on setting up the client file.

Begin keeping time in this matter for the duration of the firm's representation. See the manual and billing time guidelines provided for additional information. Time entry sheets will also be provided. Your supervising attorney will explain the distinction between "billable" and "non-billable" time.

Problem 4: Correspondence/Retainer Agreement

Draft a cover letter to send to Ms. Patton, along with the retainer agreement that has been prepared by the managing partner. Sample correspondence can be found in the forms bank. Review the retainer agreement. Submit a copy of your cover letter to your supervising attorney for review. Be sure to follow the firm's guidelines on professional communications and keep track of your billable time.

Problem 5: Commencement of Representation of Audrey Patton

Once Ms. Patton has returned a signed copy of the retainer agreement, which will be provided to you by your supervising attorney, update the client file accordingly, including the last couple of pages of the Client Intake Questionnaire. Also update the Checklist for Opening Files.

In addition, Ms. Patton has provided multiple files that need to be reviewed in connection with her case. Review all the client files that have been provided to you and begin filing documents in the appropriate sections of your client binder. Update the File Index Form with documents as they are added. Make a list of questions you have about the case as you review the files. You will have a conference with your supervising attorney soon.

Don't forget to bill your time.

Problem 6: Interoffice Conference

What are your thoughts about Ms. Patton's situation? Do you think she has a case? Is there additional information you need to know before you can decide? Meet with your supervising attorney and other team members to discuss Ms. Patton's case and all the documentation that has been provided to the firm. Also, review the retainer agreement to determine whether you can bill Ms. Patton for the time spent in an interoffice conference. If the time is billable, be sure to update your time entry. Ask your supervising attorney if you have any questions or concerns.

Problem 7: Rule 11 and Witness Interviews

Rules of Civil Procedure and ethical norms require attorneys to conduct reasonable inquiry into the facts and law prior to filing suit. Attorneys must not file cases for which there is no evidentiary support. Put another way, an attorney cannot pursue a suit that is not objectively reasonable based on the facts, else he or she runs the risk of receiving a Rule 11 sanction.

In a case like Ms. Patton's, there is a sense of urgency in seeking legal recourse. She does not know who is behind the fake profile or if she is in any danger. Furthermore, she has no ability without the court's assistance to unmask the anonymous online nemesis. Thus, the firm must strike a balance between expediency in filing a claim to bring relief to the client and adequate diligence in vetting the facts that have been presented by the client.

Generally, attorneys should attempt to corroborate the client's account prior to filing suit. There is no magic formula for the appropriate level of review, but it should include some combination of reviewing the details of the client's interview, interviewing witnesses identified by the client, searching for publicly available information of relevance, and reviewing the documents or other evidence within the client's possession. Ms. Patton has delivered some information to the firm, but it would be helpful to conduct some additional corroboration. Ms. Patton has suggested three potential witnesses: Dylan Burke, the managing partner of her firm; Charlie Patton, her spouse; and Taylor Cabello, the client who fired her. One of the team's paralegals conducted an interview of Dylan Burke already. A memo to file summarizing that interview can be accessed in the firm's case files. Review the memo and add a copy of it to the client's file.

Your supervising attorney will instruct you whether to prepare to interview either Charlie or Taylor. Submit your list of questions to your supervising attorney for review. Your supervising attorney will let you know when the witness interviews will be scheduled. Prepare a memo to file for each witness after each interview.

Don't forget to bill your time.

Problem 8: Researching the Potential Causes of Action

Your team needs to determine what viable causes of action Ms. Patton may have. This will require carefully analyzing the elements of each potential claim to see if Ms. Patton can satisfy the legal standards based on the facts of her case.

A research file has been provided, which contains all the relevant, potential claims Ms. Patton may be able to make. If information about a particular law is not provided in the research file, it is because that cause of action is either not recognized in your jurisdiction or because it is of a criminal nature, which is outside the scope of the work that Seymour Justice has been hired to do.

Your supervising attorney will assign the area of law you need to research. Prepare a short legal memo summarizing the required elements of the cause of action(s) you have been assigned to analyze, as well as the likelihood of success for Ms. Patton, given the facts now known. Be sure to address the statutes of limitation that apply and update the calendar/tickler accordingly.

Do not conduct any outside legal research unless instructed to do so by your supervising attorney. And remember to keep track of your billable time.

Problem 9: Interoffice Conference/Client Invoice

Review all the work you have done on Ms. Patton's case with your supervising attorney. Make sure your client file is updated with all relevant documents. Discuss your analysis and conclusions about viable causes of action. Bill your time, as applicable.

It is also time to prepare your client's first invoice for all the time billed on this matter. Each team member will prepare separate invoices, unless otherwise directed by your supervising attorney. Use the Invoice template in the forms bank as a guide.

Problem 10: Doe Defendants

Your supervising attorney is ready to move forward with preparing Ms. Patton's complaint and will advise you on what cause(s) of action you will pursue.

It may seem tricky to bring a case when you do not know whom to sue. Review the interoffice memo that was previously prepared in connection with the *Norris* case regarding Doe defendants.

Assist in preparing a complaint. A sample defamation template is available in the forms bank. Adapt it to suit the particulars of Ms. Patton's case, including, perhaps, a different cause of action. Your supervising attorney will assign the drafting portion(s) you are responsible for. Submit your drafts to your supervising attorney for review. Do not forget to keep accurate track of your billable time.

Problem 11: Unmasking Anonymous Defendants

Now that the complaint has been filed, update the client file. In addition, it is important that the firm acts quickly to learn the identity of the Doe defendant and file the Doe Amendment.

Since Rendezvous will not provide information on the anonymous user who created the fake profile without a court order/subpoena, Ms. Patton will need to pursue the court's assistance. One plausible option is to take the approach the firm used in the *Norris* case: filing a motion for early discovery. With the court's permission, Ms. Patton can seek a subpoena for Rendezvous, to require them to provide certain identifying information about Doe that would help her prepare her lawsuit and give proper notice to the defendant that he or she is being sued. In cases involving anonymity online, it can be a challenge to uncover real identities because people often do not provide 100 percent accurate information when registering for various internet services. Thus, it is often necessary to seek information, such as an internet protocol (IP) address, that companies may have access to that will help us track down the anonymous poster.

Discovery in a case can take a long time and cost a significant amount of money to complete, depending on the complexity of the case and the resources available. There can be informal discovery, such as the witness interviews your team conducted already. However, there are more formal tools of discovery in litigation as well, including interrogatories, depositions, subpoenas, and requests for documents.

Typically, the formal discovery process begins once the defendant has answered the complaint. In a case like Ms. Patton's, which involves an unknown defendant who likely does not even know of the lawsuit's existence, it is somewhat impractical to adhere to the normal timeframe or procedure for discovery. Thus, a plaintiff with a Doe defendant may seek some tools of discovery on an expedited basis. While there has been a noted increase in the granting of expedited discovery requests in the case of Doe defendants involved in allegedly bad behavior online, there is no guarantee that the court will grant the request for early discovery.

It is probably Ms. Patton's best strategy, though. Review the *Norris* motion for early discovery for information on "unmasking" anonymous internet users. Your supervising attorney will assign a section of Ms. Patton's motion for you to draft. Refer to the *Norris* motion as a guide but be careful to incorporate relevant facts from the client's file, especially her initial interview. There are many details in the transcript of the interview and supporting documents that have been provided that can help bolster Ms. Patton's motion.

Bill your time.

Problem 12: Issuing a Subpoena

Congratulations! The court granted your motion for early discovery and your supervising attorney will provide you with a copy of the order. A substantial portion of the subpoena has already been drafted for you but will need to be updated with the current date. Prepare the subpoena for delivery to Rendezvous. Also, note that per the terms of the court's order, Seymour Justice will need to include express instructions to Rendezvous in addition to the form subpoena that

1) Rendezvous shall provide notice to the individual operating under the account name Audrey_Patton_Paramour, and
2) Rendezvous shall allow the above-named individual fifteen calendar days to object before Rendezvous may release any information to Seymour Justice.

Draft a letter to Rendezvous, to be sent by certified mail, return receipt requested. Enclose a copy of the subpoena and the order. Be sure to clearly communicate the directions 1) and 2) outlined above in your letter, as ordered by the court. Contact information for Rendezvous can be found in the file.

As always, bill your time and update your client file. In addition, set a due date and a tickler on your calendar, and mark the relevant docket record in your file to remember the deadline for Rendezvous to respond to the subpoena. That return date information can be found on the subpoena.

Problem 13: Unmasking by Using an IP Address/Updating Conflict Check

The firm has received Rendezvous's response to the subpoena. They claim to not have access to all identifying information requested by the subpoena. However, they were able to provide some information that should be helpful in identifying the Doe defendant, including an IP address. Your supervising attorney asked the firm's technology department to help decode the IP information. Your supervising attorney will provide the results of that request with you. Review both the correspondence from Rendezvous and the tech department's IP look-up results. Do you have enough information to determine the true identity of Doe?

Update the conflicts screening, now that a new party has entered the matter. Run the preliminary check by reviewing the client database provided. If there is potential conflict, notify your supervising attorney immediately prior to continuing any work on the matter. If there does not appear to be a conflict based on the preliminary check, you should still submit an updated conflicts request by using the form provided. Send the updated Conflict Investigation Form to your supervising attorney, who will then submit the form to the conflicts department for processing.

Update your files with the new information. Your supervising attorney will inform Ms. Patton of this update and advise you on next steps.

Problem 14: Amending the Complaint

Now that the defendant's actual identity has been revealed, it is time to file an amendment to the complaint to update Doe's name. A template is available in the forms bank. Draft the amendment and submit to your supervising attorney for review. As always, remember to bill your time.

Problem 15: Defendant's Answer

The supervising attorney will provide you with a copy of the answer that the defendant has filed in this case. Update the files accordingly. Prepare for a status conference with your supervising attorney to discuss next steps.

Problem 16: Settlement Options

Ms. Patton has spoken to your supervising attorney about her preference to end this litigation without going trial. In part, she is worried that the nature of the case could garner unwanted media attention. Also, she believes it will be possible to reach a mutually agreeable settlement with the defendant. She would like to settle for a minimum of $25,000, though she believes her claim is probably worth at least twice that. She would like to donate the money to CyberSafeSpace, an organization that advocates for victims of cyber abuse.

Prepare a settlement demand letter that reflects the terms with which Ms. Patton would be most comfortable. The letter should include details about Ms. Patton's damages and a discussion of the defendant's liability. However, given Ms. Patton's desire for an amicable end to this dispute, avoid unnecessarily adversarial language. Submit a copy to your supervising attorney for review.

While the terms are subject to variation, the general format of the letter should be as follows:

- One to two paragraphs: provide a narrative summary about Ms. Patton. Describe her successful career, good reputation, and well-being prior to the posting on Rendezvous.
- A few paragraphs: describe the experience with the Rendezvous posting, including how she learned about it, the multiple unwanted correspondences she received, and the angry client's reaction. Be factual and include support for the details by including exhibits from the case file.
- A few paragraphs: discuss the causes of action that underlie Ms. Patton's pending complaint. Use appropriate citations for legal authorities.
- One to two paragraphs: describe Ms. Patton's damages. Include the economic impact, reputational harm, and emotional suffering.
- One to two paragraphs: provide a reasonable statement of the value of Ms. Patton's damages. This total should include lost earnings and any other calculable amount. This section should also include information regarding likely jury awards, punitive damages, etc., if any. Be as specific as possible, but do not exaggerate the amount. If there is not enough information available for you to reasonably estimate a total, flag this section of the letter as a topic needing additional client information.
- One paragraph: end with a settlement amount (the demand) and a deadline by which the defendant must respond to accept the settlement amount.

Problem 17: Interoffice Conference re: Settlement

Meet with your supervising attorney and the rest of your team for a status conference. Your supervising attorney will update you on any developments regarding settlement.

Prepare the second client invoice for time billed between Invoice 1 and the present. Submit the invoice to your supervising attorney for review.

Problem 18: Conclusion of Representation

Congratulations on the successful conclusion of the Patton case and a successful stint at Seymour Justice! Now that your time with SJ is coming to an end, you will need to ensure that all client files are updated and complete. In addition, the managing partner has required a brief interoffice memo from you describing your experience with the firm. Submit your memo and client file to your supervising attorney, who may also schedule an exit conference with you.

www.ingramcontent.com/pod-product-compliance
Lightning Source LLC
Chambersburg PA
CBHW081126180926
51611CB00004B/66
9781601568250